or
Does Father Reeeeeeally Know Best?

Adapted from Shakespeare's play

by

NANCY LINEHAN CHARLES

Dramatic Publishing
Woodstock, Illinois • England • Australia • New Zealand

*** NOTICE ***

The amateur and stock acting rights to this work are controlled exclusively by THE DRAMATIC PUBLISHING COMPANY without whose permission in writing no performance of it may be given. Royalty must be paid every time a play is performed whether or not it is presented for profit and whether or not admission is charged. A play is performed any time it is acted before an audience. Current royalty rates, applications and restrictions may be found at our Web site: www.dramaticpublishing.com, or we may be contacted by mail at: DRAMATIC PUBLISHING COMPANY, 311 Washington St., Woodstock IL 60098.

COPYRIGHT LAW GIVES THE AUTHOR OR THE AUTHOR'S AGENT THE EXCLUSIVE RIGHT TO MAKE COPIES. This law provides authors with a fair return for their creative efforts. Authors earn their living from the royalties they receive from book sales and from the performance of their work. Conscientious observance of copyright law is not only ethical, it encourages authors to continue their creative work. This work is fully protected by copyright. No alterations, deletions or substitutions may be made in the work without the prior written consent of the publisher. No part of this work may be reproduced or transmitted in any form or by any means, electronic or mechanical, including photocopy, recording, videotape, film, or any information storage and retrieval system, without permission in writing from the publisher. It may not be performed either by professionals or amateurs without payment of royalty. All rights, including, but not limited to, the professional, motion picture, radio, television, videotape, foreign language, tabloid, recitation, lecturing, publication and reading, are reserved.

For performance of any songs, music and recordings mentioned in this play which are in copyright, the permission of the copyright owners must be obtained or other songs and recordings in the public domain substituted.

©MMVIII by
NANCY LINEHAN CHARLES

Printed in the United States of America
All Rights Reserved
(HAMLET or Does Father Reeeeeally Know Best?)

ISBN: 978-1-58342-563-3

IMPORTANT BILLING AND CREDIT REQUIREMENTS

* * * *

The original production of *HAMLET or Does Father Reeeeeeally Know Best?* was made possible through the generous contributions of Pacific Resident Theatre, Venice, Calif. Thank you to Greg Parkos, Clabe and Thea Hartley, Aldis Browne, Charles Dougherty and Mary Lou Belli, Mr. and Mrs. Stephan Betz, Mr. and Mrs. Thomas Beck, Mr. and Mrs. Ronald Sherouse, Mr. and Mrs. Frank Beddor, Mr. and Mrs. Kevin Kilner.

HAMLET or Does Father Reeeeeeally Know Best? was first produced at Mark Twain Middle School in Mar Vista, Calif., on April 17, 2008. It subsequently moved to Pacific Resident Theatre in Venice on May 3, 2008, with the following cast:

Storytellers	Barbara Betancourt
	Stephanie Machado
	Brian Menjivar
Ghost of Hamlet's Father	Donna Feria
Hamlet	Elijah Atmore
Claudius	Isaiah Eisendorf
Gertrude	Abeli Hernandez
Polonius	Jacob Varela
Laertes	David Monterrubio
Ophelia	Alicia Maldonado
Marcellus	Edwin Graciano
Horatio	Brian Menjivar
Gravediggers/Players	Jasmine Daboul
	Shirley Lopez

Producer	Candi Lira
Costumes	April Clemens
Set	Norman Scott
Lighting	Fabian Rodriguez
Asst. Director/Fight Choreographer	Will Rothhaar

Directed by	Michael Rothhaar

Special thanks to: Aldis Browne, Clabe and Thea Hartley, Greg Parkos, Pacific Resident Theatre and maryjane, Kate Kausch, Mariel Roderiguez, Ricci Luca, Dr. Mary Reid, Connie Vandergriff, Ron Thiel, Ric Lira, Kent Clemens, Toni Boyette and the parents of all the actors.

ADAPTOR'S NOTE

I discovered early on that kids hear Shakespeare through their hearts. They hear it on a level to which, sadly, many adults—and often very academically accomplished adults—are tone-deaf. Someone who works on an intuitive level with Shakespeare's language explained this to me: that Shakespeare writes mostly in iambic pentameter, which rhythm sounds like a heartbeat—ba-bom, ba-bom, ba-bom. Five of these to a line. Hearing their heartbeat more clearly than perhaps us jaded adults, children respond instinctively to the song.

I began searching years ago for ways to bring the stories of Shakespeare and a good chunk of the language to children. When my younger son Will (named after Shakespeare) was in the fifth grade, I adapted *Macbeth* to the stage for a school fund-raiser. I called it *Macbeth, According to the Fifth Grade*. It was a runaway hit. So much so, we moved it to a professional venue for five weekends and made $4500 for the tiny, struggling public school that had originated the production.

I was off and running. I've since adapted five of Shakespeare's plays for kids—all published through Dramatic Publishing.

Hamlet is particularly close to my heart because at thirteen, I stumbled into a rehearsal of that play and fell instantly in love. I remember what I was wearing, I remember the texture of the carpet I was standing on. No, I didn't understand the words immediately, but it sang! I was never the same again. I fell for acting and Shakespeare in the same instant and knew what I wanted to do with my life.

I know this stuff works. I've had the supreme pleasure of watching kindergartners race to the playground to gather sticks from Birnham Wood and prepare to slay the evil Macbeth—right after hearing the Bard's story. I've heard middle-schoolers quoting Iago in the hallway between classes; and one teenage girl at her locker in a south central Los Angeles high school was heard to rebuff her boyfriend with Hermia's exact words to Lysander in *Midsummer Night's Dream*: LIE....FURTHER...OFF!!!

If I could be the lady who brought Shakespeare to kids, I would die a happy woman!

HAMLET
or Does Father Reeeeeally Know Best?

CHARACTERS

HAMLET . . . . prince of Denmark

CLAUDIUS . Hamlet's uncle and current king of Denmark

GERTRUDE . . . . Hamlet's mother and queen of Denmark

OLD HAMLET (GHOST). . . . . . former king of Denmark:
Hamlet's father

POLONIUS . . . . . . old, trusted advisor to Danish Royalty;
a little dotty

LAERTES . . . . a college student and son of Polonius

OPHELIA . . . . . daughter of Polonius and sister of Laertes

HORATIO. . . . . Hamlet's best friend from college

MARCELLUS . . . . a soldier in the castle

2 PLAYERS

2 GUARDS/2 GRAVEDIGGERS (played by the same
actors, if need be)

3 STORYTELLERS (can be male or female: the names
can be changed)

Cross-gender casting is possible and, indeed, encouraged. Only Hamlet and Claudius should be male; Ophelia and Gertrude should be female. Everyone else can be cross-cast, gender-wise. We usually cast everyone who auditions—what castle couldn't use a few more courtiers?

The play takes place at Elsinore Castle in Denmark.

HAMLET
or Does Father Reeeeeeally Know Best?

AT RISE: *As the audience enters the school or theatre lobby, there is a GHOST wandering among them. The GHOST should be wearing a helmet (see back notes to learn how to make a cheap helmet out of a plastic gallon milk container) and have a sword on his belt. He is wearing very white make-up. He should be on the edges of the room or crowd to begin with, but as they gather, he should be more obvious. He never speaks. When the house is ready to open, the GHOST should beckon the audience in. Always silently.*

First Storyteller (SAMANTHA) is standing downstage center with her hands on her hips, looking at the audience as they come in. Two other Storytellers (ERIC and JEN) flank her.

SAM. Well, come on in, come on in. Don't be shy. Don't pay any attention to him *(indicating the GHOST)*. He was a king, but he's dead. Just take your seats and we'll get started. Here! We'll give you a hand.

(All three STORYTELLERS jump down off the stage and whistle back toward the wings.)

9

STORYTELLERS. Come on, you guys. Lend a hand here.

(Out from the wings stream all the actors, dressed variously as soldiers, a student (HAMLET), a king (CLAUDIUS), a queen (GERTRUDE), an old man (POLONIUS), a young girl with flowers in her hair (OPHELIA), a young man with a briefcase or book satchel (LAERTES), etc. And the GHOST wanders through them all. They go about helping the audience to their seats, chatting, showing a bit of mild swordplay here and there. Whenever the GHOST passes the players, they stop talking and kneel before him...then stand up and watch him pass, shaking their heads.

When all the audience is seated, we hear another whistle from SAM. All the players make their way back to the stage and off into the wings. The Ghost (OLD HAMLET), CLAUDIUS, GERTRUDE and YOUNG HAMLET remain on stage, standing downstage right—GERTRUDE hanging on CLAUDIUS, HAMLET looking dark and sullen, the GHOST standing silently. Downstage left stands POLONIUS, LAERTES and OPHELIA.

SAM *(to the audience)*. Well done!!! You guys are an orderly bunch. Mostly. It's a good thing because the story we're gonna tell you tonight is anything BUT orderly.
ERIC. The guy who told us the story is named William Shakespeare. Ever heard of him?

(If the audience sits there silently, JEN says:)

JEN. Well, don't just sit there being orderly. Really. HAVE you ever heard of William Shakespeare?

(The STORYTELLERS then prod the audience for a response.)

SAM. Well, all right then. That's better. For those of you who don't know him, he wrote plays.

JEN. And then he died.

ERIC. Well, not BECAUSE he wrote plays.

SAM. He just got old. But this guy was one HECK of a storyteller. He lived about 400 years ago...

JEN. But we won't hold that against him.

ERIC. So. The story we're gonna tell you tonight is about THIS guy.

(HAMLET waves sullenly to the audience.)

SAM. His name is Hamlet, and if you check your program closely, you'll see he's the main guy. You can tell 'cause Shakespeare named the play after him.

JEN. That's his mother, Gertrude *(GERTRUDE waves)* and his uncle Claudius *(CLAUDIUS salutes)* and his father, Old Hamlet, who's dead but still has a few things to say.

OLD HAMLET
     Boo!

ERIC. The story takes place in Denmark.

SAM. But Shakespeare didn't stop with just ONE dysfunctional Danish family. He wrote about this other family as well. There's old, wise, dotty Polonius, who's an ad-

viser to the king and queen *(POLONIUS waves)* ...
Ophelia, his daughter, who used to be kinda Hamlet's
girlfriend *(OPHELIA curtsies)* and Laertes, his son
(LAERTES bows briskly to the audience).

JEN. So, see...this story is basically about these two fami-
lies.

ERIC. Let's all say their names together so we'll remember
them as the story goes along.

ALL THREE STORYTELLERS. Hamlet.

(HAMLET waves again.)

AUDIENCE. Hamlet.

*(The STORYTELLERS go through each character's
name, always prodding the audience to participate by
repeating the name. If they're slow to do it, SAM says
something like:)*

SAM. Wha'd'ja think? You're gonna get a free ride here?
Speak up!!

*(After the name recitation, HORATIO comes onto the
stage.)*

SAM. Oh!! We forgot someone. This is Horatio, Hamlet's
best friend from college. I don't wanta spoil it for you,
but he's the only guy left standing at the end of this
play, so remember his face.

(HORATIO comes downstage center and pushes his face out to the audience. Then does profiles so the audience will remember.)

ERIC. OK. So say his name. Don't be shy: Horatio.
AUDIENCE. Horatio.
JEN. I've never seen a cuter audience. One more thing. Sometimes in our play, girls will be pretending to be boys. Don't get bent out of shape. In Shakespeare's day BOYS played ALL the parts.
SAM. So it's payback!!
ERIC. All right, actors: PLACES!!!

(All the actors run into the wings. The three STORY-TELLERS take their places on various levels of step ladders. Two actors, who will act as SOLDIERS to the king, come on stage carrying two chairs—fancy chairs to look like two thrones. CLAUDIUS and GERTRUDE sit on these. The SOLDIERS stand to the side. HAMLET lies on the floor with a book...his back to his mother and stepfather.)

JEN. To begin with, the old King Hamlet has just died and right away, Hamlet's mother Gertrude marries her dead husband's brother Claudius.
ERIC. Like before you can blink. Whamo! Here's what Hamlet says about that.

HAMLET
    Thrift, thrift... The funeral baked meats
    Did coldly furnish forth the marriage tables.

JEN. Cool. The way he talks, huh? So anyway, Claudius, Hamlet's uncle, becomes king. And Hamlet thinks there's something fishy goin' on. And he gets real gloomy about it. And the new king and queen keep buggin' Hamlet to snap out of it. Put on a happy face.

CLAUDIUS
> Now Hamlet… How is it that the clouds still hang on you?

GERTRUDE
> Good Hamlet, cast thy nighted color off,
> And let thine eye look like a friend on Denmark.

CLAUDIUS
> We pray you, throw to earth
> This unprevailing woe and think of US
> *(CLAUDIUS indicates himself.)*
> As of a father.

GERTRUDE
> Hamlet, I pray thee, stay with us.
> Go not to Wittenburg.

ERIC. That's Hamlet's college.

HAMLET *(sullenly)*
> I shall in all my best obey you, Madame.

(The KING and QUEEN, the chairs and actors, go off stage. HAMLET stands alone.)

HAMLET

> O, that this too, too solid flesh would melt,
> Thaw, and resolve itself into a dew.
> That it should come to this:
> But two months dead—nay, not so much, not two.
> Within a month—a little month—she married with
> my uncle.
> My father's brother, but no more like my father
> Than I to Hercules.
> But break my heart, for I must hold my tongue.

SAM. But then his best friend Horatio comes in to tell him
that he's seen Old Hamlet—the ghost of Hamlet's dad,
the guy you just saw in the lobby—wandering around on
the battlements of the castle.

*(During SAM's last speech, HAMLET walks around the
center of the stage with HORATIO, and the latter panto-
mimes telling him about seeing the GHOST.)*

HAMLET

> I will watch tonight.
> Perchance 'twill walk again.
> I'll speak to it, though hell itself should gape
> And bid me hold my peace.

(HORATIO bows to HAMLET and walks off.)

HAMLET

> My father's spirit in arms! All is not well.
> I doubt some foul play. *(HAMLET runs off stage.)*

SAM. Meantime...Laertes is about to go off to college. He's packed up his clothes and his i-Pod *(or i-Mac or i-Phone or whatever's hip)* and now he's talking to his little sister Ophelia. Giving her the old brotherly advice.

LAERTES
    For Hamlet, and the trifling of his favor...
    Perhaps he loves you now,
    But you must fear; his will is not his own.
    Then keep you in the rear of your affection,
    Out of the shot and danger of desire.

OPHELIA
    I shall the effect of this good lesson keep
    As watchman to my heart.

    (POLONIUS comes toward them.)

POLONIUS
    Yet here, Laertes? There, my blessing with thee.
    Be thou familiar, but by no means vulgar.

ERIC. Oh boy. Now Laertes gets the advice.

POLONIUS
    Neither a borrower nor a lender be,
    For loan oft loses both itself and friend.
    This above all: to thine own self be true,
    And it must follow, as the night the day,
    Thou canst not then be false to any man.
    Farewell. My blessing season this in thee.

LAERTES
> Most humbly do I take my leave, my lord.
> Farewell, Ophelia, and remember well
> What I have said to you.

OPHELIA
> 'Tis in my memory locked,
> And you yourself shall keep the key of it.

(LAERTES exits. POLONIUS looks at OPHELIA.)

POLONIUS
> What is it, Ophelia, he hath said to you?

OPHELIA
> So please you, something touching the Lord Hamlet.

POLONIUS
> Ah! 'Tis told me he hath very oft of late
> Given private time to you...

ALL THREE STORYTELLERS. UH-OH!!!

OPHELIA
> He hath, my lord, of late made many tenders
> Of his affection to me.

POLONIUS
> Affection, puh!!!!

SAM. Did you hear that? Puh!! It's that kinda thing makes you know, Shakespeare is right down there in the street with the rest of us. Puh!!

POLONIUS
>From this time,
Be something scanter of your maiden presence.
Do not believe his vows.
Give not words or talk with the Lord Hamlet.

OPHELIA
I shall obey, my lord.

(OPHELIA and POLONIUS exit.)

JEN. See...nobody argued with their dad back then. No. I think dads are more reasonable today. Let's hear it for our dads!!

(STORYTELLERS goad the audience into cheering the dads in the house.)

ERIC. Meanwhile, back on the parapets of the castle, Hamlet and Horatio and another soldier, Marcellus, are keeping the watch and looking for the ghost of Hamlet's father.

(Indeed, HAMLET, HORATIO and MARCELLUS come on stage with swords drawn.)

SAM. It's getting late and they've been wandering around the castle fortress for hours with no luck.

ERIC. And nothin' to eat.
SAM & JEN. Shhhhhh!

(The GHOST drifts onto the stage.)

HORATIO
> Look, my lord, it comes.

HAMLET
> Angels and ministers of grace, defend us!
> Be thou a spirit of health or goblin damned,
> I will speak to thee. I'll call thee "Hamlet,"
> "King," "Father," "Royal Dane." O, answer me!

(The GHOST beckons for HAMLET to follow him.)

HAMLET
> It will not speak. Then I will follow it.

HORATIO
> Do not, my lord.

HAMLET
> Why, what should be the fear?
> I do not set my life at a pin's fee.
> It waves me forth again. I'll follow it.

MARCELLUS
> You shall not go, my lord.

(MARCELLUS and HORATIO grab HAMLET and try to hold him back.)

HAMLET
>   Hold off your hands!
>   By heaven, I'll make a ghost of him that lets me!
>   I say, away!
>   *(To the GHOST.)*
>   Go on... I'll follow thee.

(He throws the two men off and follows the GHOST off stage.)

HORATIO
>   He waxes desperate with imagination.

MARCELLUS
>   Let's follow.
>   Something is rotten in the state of Denmark.

(HORATIO and MARCELLUS chase after them. The STORYTELLERS jump down from their ladders.)

ERIC. Well, Hamlet's friends don't want to leave him alone with a ghost. I mean, what are friends for?

SAM. But now that old spirit is about to blow Hamlet's mind.

(The GHOST leads HAMLET back onto the stage, downstage center.)

JEN. See...he tells him things about Claudius that Hamlet has suspected already. But what makes it all so hard to ignore, is that it's a GHOST that's doing the telling.

GHOST
> Now Hamlet, hear.
> 'Tis given out that, sleeping in my orchard,
> A serpent stung me. But know, thou noble youth,
> The serpent that did sting thy father's life
> Now wears his crown.

HAMLET
> O, my prophetic soul! My uncle!

GHOST
> Brief let me be. Sleeping within my orchard,
> Upon my secure hour, thy uncle stole,
> With juice of cur-sed hebona in a vial,
> And in the porches of my ears did pour
> The leprous distillment...

ALL THREE STORYTELLERS. He...means...POISON!!
JEN. Like his brother poured it in his EAR!!!! Eeeeuuuuu-
    wwwww!!!!

GHOST
> Thus was I, sleeping, by a brother's hand
> Of life, of crown, of queen at once dispatched,
> Cut off. If thou hast nature in thee, bear it not.
> But, however thou pursues this act,
> Taint not thy mind against thy mother.
> Leave her to heaven and to those thorns
> That prick and sting her. Fare thee well.
> Remember me.

(The GHOST drifts off stage.)

SAM. And then he's gone. And then…Hamlet goes ballis-
tic!

HAMLET
     REMEMBER THEE!!???
     Ay, thou poor ghost. REMEMBER THEE?
     Yea, from the table of my memory
     I'll wipe away all trivial, fond records
     That youth and observation copied there,
     And thy commandment all alone shall live
     Within the book and volume of my brain.
     O villain, villain, smiling, dam-ned villain!
     So, uncle, there you are. I have sworn it.

*(HAMLET wanders around the stage, pulling at his own
hair, acting goofy, babbling. HORATIO and MARCEL-
LUS run on and observe this behavior.)*

ERIC. And right away, Hamlet starts to act a little goofy.
Well, come on. Chatting with the ghost of your dad is
bound to leave you a little wacky.

HORATIO
     These are but wild and whirling words, my lord.

HAMLET
     I am sorry they offend you.

HORATIO
     There's no offense, my lord.

HAMLET
> But there is, Horatio,
> And much offense, too.
> It is an honest ghost.
> Give me one poor request.

HORATIO
> What is it, my lord. We will.

HAMLET
> Never make known what you have seen tonight.

HORATIO/MARCELLUS
> My lord, we will not.

HAMLET *(pulling out his sword)*
> Swear it. Upon my sword.

GHOST *(leaning out from the wings, whispering)*
> Swear.

HAMLET *(seeing the GHOST, which HORATIO and MARCELLUS can't see)*
> Ha, ha, boy, sayst thou so?
> *(To his friends.)*
> SWEAR by my sword!!

GHOST
> Swear by his sword.

HAMLET *(to the GHOST)*
> Well said, old mole.

HORATIO
    O day and night, but this is wondrous strange.

HAMLET
    There are more things in heaven and earth, Horatio,
    Than are dreamt of in your philosophy.
    Swear on my sword.

GHOST *(whispering loudly)*
    Swear.

(HAMLET holds out his sword and both his friends put their hands on the blade.)

HAMLET
    Rest, rest, pertur-bed spirit.
    The time is out of joint. O cur-sed spite,
    That ever I was born to set it right!

(All three men leave together.)

SAM. OK. So there it is: Hamlet's father has said Hamlet must kill his uncle—because his uncle did that to him—the ghost.

ERIC. This was a kind of early time before there were courts and lawyers. Maybe there were even dinosaurs back then.

JEN *(to ERIC)*. You sound as crazy as Hamlet.

ERIC. Whatever… Hamlet is now set on killing his uncle to revenge his father.

SAM. And he decides that until he gets a plan figured out, he'll just act crazy.

JEN. He'll put an "antic disposition" on. So people will think, "Oh, that's just wacky Hamlet, crazy with grief over his father."

ERIC. Ophelia even thinks Hamlet has lost it. She tells her dad.

(OPHELIA and POLONIUS come walking on stage. OPHELIA is obviously upset.)

OPHELIA

    Lord Hamlet, with his doublet all unbraced,
    No hat upon his head, his knees knocking each other,
    He comes before me.

POLONIUS

    Mad for thy love?

OPHELIA

    My lord, I do not know,
    But truly I do fear it.

POLONIUS

    What said he?

OPHELIA

    He took me by the wrist and held me hard.
    Then raised a sigh so piteous and profound
    As it did seem to shatter all his bulk
    And end his being. That done, he lets me go,
    And, with his head over his shoulder turned,
    He seemed to find his way without his eyes,

For out of doors he went without their helps
And to the last, bended their light on me.

POLONIUS
Come, go with me. I will go seek the king.
This is the very ecstacy of love.

(POLONIUS and OPHELIA exit.)

JEN. So old Polonius thinks that his advice to his daughter
Ophelia to ignore Hamlet's come-ons...he thinks this
has driven Hamlet crazy.

SAM. So he's going to ask the king to spy on Hamlet and
Ophelia to see if this is the reason.

JEN. This would make me scream if my dad did this to
me. But dads got better as the centuries rolled on by.

ERIC. Moving on. Hamlet is acting all goofy and at the
same time, he's trying to figure out a way to PROVE
that his uncle killed his father.

SAM. 'Cause...like...he doesn't fully trust...A GHOST!!!
Duuuuh!!!

JEN. So, just about then, a troupe of actors come to the
castle. See, actors back then didn't have a HOME to
perform in, like we have this auditorium, or cafeteria, or
cafetorium. Whatever.

ERIC. They had to just roll on down the road until they
bumped into a castle.

SAM. Then they'd maybe do a play there. For the king and
queen.

ERIC. And wha'd'ya know? The players bump into Elsinore!! And Hamlet gets an idea. He'll put a speech into

their play about murdering a king in an orchard by pouring poison in his ear.

JEN. Sound familiar? He wants to see his uncle's reaction.

(HAMLET comes on stage with a PLAYER, who has a jester hat on.)

HAMLET

>Can you play "The Murder of Gonzago"?

PLAYER

>Ay, my lord.

HAMLET

>We'll have it tomorrow night. You could study a speech of some dozen or sixteen lines, which I would set down and insert in it, could you not?

PLAYER

>Ay, my lord.

HAMLET

>Very well. Speak the speech, I pray you...trippingly on the tongue; but if you mouth it, as many of our players do, I had as lief the town crier spoke my lines. Nor do not saw the air too much with your hand, thus...

(The actor playing HAMLET flails around with his hands.)

HAMLET
   …but use all gently.

(SAM drags out a picture of the Globe Theatre…the one with the hole in the roof.)

SAM. All right, now this is cool. See this hole in this theatre. Well, in Shakespeare's day, it was believed that it was part of an actor's job to say his words with honesty. And they would fly up through this hole and into the sky and outer space and help the planets turn in their orbits. But if they hammed it up…the planets might crash into each other and…DOOMSDAY!!!!! Tell that one to your history teacher. She'll LOVE you.

ERIC. So Hamlet tells the player: DON'T BE A HAM BONE!!!

JEN. Well…the player says OK and leaves, and then Hamlet's by himself. He's kinda down on himself because he hasn't acted yet on his father's command.

HAMLET
   O, what a rogue and peasant slave am I.
   Fie on't, ah fie!
   I am pigeon-livered and lack gall
   To make oppression bitter.
   I have heard that guilty creatures sitting at a play
   Have, by the very cunning of the scene,
   Been struck so to the soul that presently
   They have proclaimed their malefactions.
   For murder, though it have no tongue, will speak
   With most miraculous organ.

I'll have grounds more relative than this.
The play's the thing
Wherein I'll catch the conscience...of the king!!

SAM. So, waiting around for the play to start, Hamlet wanders around the castle being nutty and kinda mumbling to himself so people will continue to think he's crazy.
ERIC. I have a cousin like that.
JEN. Hamlet says things about suicide.
SAM. Yikes!

HAMLET

To be...or not to be—that is the question.
To die, to sleep—
To sleep, perchance to dream. Ay, there's the rub.
For in that sleep of death what dreams may come,
When we have shuffled off this mortal coil,
Must give us pause.
Who would fardels bear,
To grunt and sweat under a weary life,
But that the dread of something after death,
Makes us rather bear those ills we have
Than fly to others that we know not of.
Thus conscience does make cowards of us all.
Soft you now, the fair Ophelia.

(As OPHELIA comes on, so do CLAUDIUS and POLONIUS, carrying ferns in front of them to hide. They peek out from behind to spy on OPHELIA and HAMLET. POLONIUS has an oversized pair of binoculars, through which he stares at the couple.)

HAMLET
    I did love you once.

OPHELIA
    Indeed, my lord, you made me believe so.

HAMLET
    You should not have believed me; I loved you not.

OPHELIA
    I was the more deceived.

(HAMLET shouts at her.)

HAMLET
    GET…THEE…TO…A…NUNNERY!!!!!

(HAMLET exits. OPHELIA cries; her father and CLAU-DIUS throw their ferns aside.)

CLAUDIUS
    Love? His affections do not that way tend.
    Madness in great ones must not unwatched go.

(They all exit the stage.)

ERIC. So…the king's a little nervous. He's afraid Hamlet is onto something. But he agrees to go to the play.

(Suddenly there's music and everyone [the castle people and the players] comes on stage, dancing and doing cartwheels and laughing and chasing each other. They

*all settle into places around a circle—which is the stage.
HAMLET sits with OPHELIA, across the circle from
CLAUDIUS and GERTRUDE. While the STORY-
TELLERS describe it, the players play out the scene.)*

SAM. So the players begin acting out this plot that Hamlet
has written for them.

*(We see a king come on stage and lie down under a tree.
A man comes up behind him and looks around furtively.
Then he takes a vial of poison from his cape and pours
the liquid in the king's ear.)*

HAMLET *(to CLAUDIUS and GERTRUDE)*
He poisons him in the garden of his estate. The man
poisoned is named Gonzago. You shall see anon how
the murderer gets the love of Gonzago's wife.

*(Suddenly CLAUDIUS jumps up and looks guiltily
about.)*

OPHELIA
The king rises.

GERTRUDE
How fares my lord?

KING
Give me some light. Away!

POLONIUS
Lights, lights, lights!!!

(Everyone runs off but HAMLET and HORATIO.)

HAMLET
> Oh, good Horatio, I'll take the ghost's word.
> Didst perceive?

HORATIO
> Very well, my lord.

HAMLET
> Upon the talk of the poisoning?

HORATIO
> I did very well note him.

HAMLET
> Soft, now to my mother.
> I will speak daggers to her, but use none.
> Leave me, friend.

(HORATIO exits. HAMLET is alone.)

HAMLET
> 'Tis now the very witching time of night,
> When churchyards yawn and hell itself breathes out
> Contagion to this world. Now could I drink hot blood
> And do such bitter business as the day
> Would quake to look on.

(POLONIUS enters, a bit out of sorts.)

POLONIUS
My lord, the queen would speak with you, and
presently.

HAMLET
Then I will come to my mother by and by.

POLONIUS
I will say so.

HAMLET
"By and by" is easily said.

(HAMLET exits. CLAUDIUS wanders on, distracted.)

POLONIUS
My lord, he's going to his mother's closet.
Behind the arras…

ALL THREE STORYTELLERS. "ARRAS" means "TAP-
ESTRY"!!

POLONIUS
Behind the arras I'll convey myself
To hear the process.
I'll call upon you ere you go to bed
And tell you what I know.

CLAUDIUS
Thanks, dear my lord.

(POLONIUS leaves. CLAUDIUS weeps, then kneels and puts his hands together in prayer.)

CLAUDIUS

> O, my offense is rank, it smells to heaven:
> A brother's murder!

ALL THREE STORYTELLERS. Gasp!!! *(They make the sound.)* The Ghost Was Right!!!!

CLAUDIUS

> What form of prayer can serve my turn?
> "Forgive me my foul murder?"
> That cannot be, since I am still possessed
> Of those effects for which I did the murder:
> My crown, mine own ambition, and my queen.
> Bow, stubborn knees!

(CLAUDIUS falls to his knees. He's lost in prayer. HAMLET enters, upstage of CLAUDIUS [behind him].)

HAMLET

> Now might I do it, now he is praying.

(He draws his sword.)

STORYTELLERS *(Gasp!)*

(HAMLET pauses as though to plunge his sword into CLAUDIUS.)

HAMLET
>And so he goes to heaven.
>A villain kills my father, and for that,
>I, his sole son, do this villain send to heaven.
>No. Up sword.
>When he is drunk asleep, or in his rage,
>Then trip him, that his heels may kick at heaven,
>And that his soul may be as damned and black
>As hell, whereto it goes.
>My mother waits.

(HAMLET runs off.)

CLAUDIUS
>My words fly up, my thoughts remain below;
>Words without thoughts never to heaven go.

(CLAUDIUS rises and exits.)

ERIC. Look, I'm as much against violence as the next guy, but we can't leave here until Hamlet kills his uncle.

SAM. That's just how it is.

ERIC. And Hamlet had a chance right then!! Did'ja see that? I mean, I got homework to do. I can't stay here all night.

SAM & JEN. Homework. Riiiiiiiight.

ERIC. OK, OK. So Hamlet goes to see his mother because she's upset about what the players did—The Murder of Gonzago, and all.

(GERTRUDE walks on stage and paces.)

SAM. And don't forget, Polonius is gonna spy on them...
JEN. AGAIN!!!!!... Nosey old guy.
ERIC. Polonius is gonna hide behind the... *(to the audience)* what was it called?

(The STORYTELLERS prod until the audience says "AR-RAS.")

ERIC. Good job!! You guys are speaking Elizabethan English, ya know.

(POLONIUS then comes on stage holding a rug-like piece of material in front of him. This is the arras—the tapestry. He waves to the audience. HAMLET comes on stage.)

HAMLET
    Now, mother, what's the matter?

GERTRUDE
    Hamlet, thou hast thy father much offended.

HAMLET
    Mother YOU have my father much offended.

GERTRUDE *(angry at his insult)*
    Have you forgot me?

HAMLET
    No. You are the queen, your husband's brother's wife,
    And (would it were not so) you are my mother.

ALL THREE STORYTELLERS. Harsh!!!

*(GERTRUDE is hurt and starts to leave. HAMLET grabs
her and sits her down. GERTRUDE shouts for help.)*

GERTRUDE
  Help ho!!!!

POLONIUS *(from behind the arras)*
  What ho! Help!

HAMLET
  How now, a rat? Dead for a ducat, dead.

*(He kills POLONIUS by thrusting his sword through the
arras. [See endnotes about doing all fight sequences
safely.] POLONIUS falls.)*

POLONIUS
  O, I am slain!

HAMLET
  Is it the king?

GERTRUDE
  O, what a rash and bloody deed is this!

HAMLET
  A bloody deed—almost as bad, good mother,
  As kill a king and marry with his brother.

GERTRUDE
    As kill a king?

HAMLET
    Ay, lady, it was my word.

(HAMLET pulls the arras off POLONIUS' body.)

HAMLET
    Thou wretched, rash, intruding fool, farewell.
    I took thee for thy better.

*(Then HAMLET grabs GERTRUDE by the shoulders
and tells her [in pantomime] what he knows from the
GHOST. He's very angry.)*

SAM. So Hamlet lets her have it. He tells her how his un-
    cle killed his father and accuses her of marrying a mur-
    derer.
JEN. This guy doesn't mince words.
ERIC. Man! My mom would ground me for a month if I
    talked to her like that.

GERTRUDE
    Oh, Hamlet, speak no more!
    These words, like daggers, enter in my ears.
    No more, sweet Hamlet.

(HAMLET shakes her. The GHOST enters.)

JEN. Uh-oh. Awkward. Hamlet can see the ghost; his
    mother can't.

HAMLET *(to the GHOST)*
> Save me and hover o'er me with your wings.

GERTRUDE
> Alas, he's mad.

GHOST
> Do not forget. This visitation
> Is but to whet thy almost blunted purpose.

ERIC. Ya see? Even a GHOST knows that Hamlet needs to GET ON WITH IT!! Do ghosts have homework too?

GHOST
> Speak to her, Hamlet.

HAMLET *(to GERTRUDE, indicating the GHOST)*
> Look you how pale he glares.

GERTRUDE
> To whom do you speak this?

HAMLET
> Do you see nothing there?

GERTRUDE
> Nothing at all; yet all that is, I see

HAMLET
> Look where he goes even now out at the portal.

(The GHOST exits.)

HAMLET
> It is not madness that I have uttered.
> Mother, for love of grace, confess yourself to heaven.
> Repent what's past, avoid what is to come.

GERTRUDE
> O Hamlet, thou hast cleft my heart in twain!

HAMLET
> O, throw away the worser part of it,
> And live the purer with the other half.
> Good night. For this same lord...
> *(He points to POLONIUS.)*
> ...I do repent.
> I will bestow him and will answer well
> The death I gave him. So again, good night.
> I must be cruel only to be kind.

(GERTRUDE and HAMLET hug.)

SAM. So Hamlet tells her to tell King Claudius that Hamlet's not really mad but seems to have some method behind his madness.

(HAMLET drags POLONIUS off stage. GERTRUDE exits.)

ERIC. So the king is upset with Hamlet when he hears that he's killed Polonius, and besides...no one seems to be able to locate the body. So, he calls Hamlet in.

(CLAUDIUS and two ATTENDANTS enter...HAMLET comes in.)

CLAUDIUS
    Now, Hamlet, where's Polonius?

HAMLET
    At supper.

CLAUDIUS
    At supper where?

HAMLET.
    Not where he eats, but where he is eaten. A certain convocation of politic worms are even at him.

CLAUDIUS
    WHERE...IS...POLONIUS?????

HAMLET
    In heaven. Send thither to see. If your messenger find him not there, seek him in the other place yourself. But if, indeed, you find him not within this month, you shall *nose* him as you go up the stairs into the lobby.

(CLAUDIUS motions the ATTENDANTS to go check where HAMLET indicated. They run off.)

CLAUDIUS
    Hamlet...this deed, for thy safety
    Must send thee hence for England.

HAMLET
    For England?

CLAUDIUS
    Ay, Hamlet. Therefore, prepare thyself.

(Both exit.)

ERIC. The plot thickens. Claudius SAYS he's sending
    Hamlet to England because Hamlet committed the crime
    of murder and he's protecting him by sending him away.

SAM. But secretly, he wants Hamlet dead, so he's sending
    him off with these two old buddies of Hamlet... Rosen-
    crantz and Guildenstern.

ERIC. Look we've mostly left them out of this because
    their names are too hard to pronounce.

SAM. But a guy named Tom Stoppard wrote a whole play
    JUST about them. It's called...

ERIC & JEN. ...ROSENCRANTZ AND GUILDEN-
    STERN ARE DEAD!

SAM. So go see THAT one if you're so interested in those
    two.

ERIC. What we CAN tell you is that the king has bought
    them off and hired them to have Hamlet killed when
    they reach England.

JEN. With friends like that, who needs enemies?

*(Suddenly OPHELIA dashes onto the stage with her
clothes all torn and flowers falling out of her hair.
GERTRUDE follows her.)*

SAM. Meanwhile, Ophelia's crazy with grief over the death of her dad.

OPHELIA
Where is the beauteous Majesty of Denmark?

GERTRUDE
How now, Ophelia.

OPHELIA *(singing and tossing flowers around)*
He is dead and gone, lady,
He is dead and gone.
At his head a grass-green turf,
At his heels a stone.

(CLAUDIUS enters.)

GERTRUDE
Alas, look here, my lord.

CLAUDIUS *(to OPHELIA)*
How do you, pretty lady?

OPHELIA
I hope all will be well. But I cannot choose but weep to think they would lay him in the cold ground. My brother shall know of it!! Good night, ladies. Good night, sweet ladies. Good night, good night. *(Exits.)*

CLAUDIUS
O, this is the poison of deep grief. It springs all from her father's death.

(To GERTRUDE.)
    Follow her close; give her good watch.

(GERTRUDE exits, following OPHELIA.)

ERIC. And before you can say "what the heck!", Laertes comes back from school to get revenge on whoever killed HIS father.

JEN. Revenge is the hot topic in Denmark.

SAM. You'd think it was an episode of the *Sopranos*.

LAERTES *(angry)*
    Where is my father?

CLAUDIUS
    Dead.

LAERTES
    How came he dead; I'll not be juggled with.

(OPHELIA comes in again, worse than ever, singing and throwing flowers, her hair all undone, her clothes rumpled.)

LAERTES
    O heat, dry up my brains!
    Dear maid, kind sister, sweet Ophelia!

OPHELIA
    Fare you well, my dove.
    There's rosemary, that's for remembrance.

Pray you, love, remember. And there is pansies,
that's for thoughts.

LAERTES
A document in madness.

OPHELIA
I would give you some violets, but they withered all
when my father died.
(Singing.)
And will he not come again?
And will he not come again?
No, no, he is dead.
Go to thy deathbed.
He never will come again.

*(OPHELIA exits, followed by GERTRUDE. LAERTES
weeps. CLAUDIUS consoles him, walks him around,
talks to him.)*

SAM. So Claudius tells Laertes who DID kill his father.

CLAUDIUS
Hamlet!

*(CLAUDIUS and LAERTES stop suddenly, and LAER-
TES GASPS!!!)*

JEN. He's shocked and wants...what else?...
ALL THREE STORYTELLERS. REVENGE!!
ERIC. Claudius says, *(the actor speaks this like a mafioso
godfather)* ...Hey, looky here, buddy boy. I know a guy.

I'll arrange it so you can have a sword fight with Hamlet, only on the tip of YOUR sword will be a surprise—a kinda potion. A kinda poison, don'tcha know. A strong one—like I say, I know a guy. One scratch, it'll kill him. Leave it to me.

SAM. Laertes agrees and all of a sudden...MORE bad news!

GERTRUDE
　　　One woe doth tread upon another's heel,
　　　So fast they follow. Your sister's drowned, Laertes.

LAERTES
　　　Drowned? O, where?

GERTRUDE
　　　There is a willow grows askant the brook,
　　　And on the pendant boughs,
　　　Her weedy trophies and herself
　　　Fell in the weeping brook.
　　　And her garments, heavy with their drink,
　　　Pulled the poor wretch from her melodious lay
　　　To muddy death.

LAERTES
　　　Too much of water hast thou, poor Ophelia,
　　　And therefore I forbid my tears. *(He runs off.)*

CLAUDIUS
　　　Let's follow, Gertrude.

(CLAUDIUS and GERTRUDE exit. The three STORY-TELLERS jump off their ladders and start grabbing tombstones from off stage, setting up a graveyard as they talk.)

JEN. So then we hear that Hamlet has escaped the ship bound for England and is headed back toward Elsinore.

SAM. He doesn't know Ophelia's dead or that Laertes is gunning for him.

ERIC. But while we wait for Hamlet to return, Shakespeare writes a scene between two gravediggers.

JEN. These are the low comics. Shakespeare puts some people like this in every play...

SAM. Even his greatest tragedies.

ERIC. Something for everyone. 'Cause there was no TV back then. Or Gameboy. Or Tivo.

JEN. Not even movies. Like...this was it. The ONLY entertainment.

SAM. So EVERYBODY came to see the plays. And low humor was popular—like the *Three Stooges*...or *South Park*.

(The GRAVEDIGGERS come on looking filthy, with shovels in their hands. If possible, teeth blacked out. They smile vacantly at the audience. They begin shoveling invisible dirt.)

ERIC. These two geniuses are having an argument about whether Ophelia killed herself or just fell in the river by accident. One of them explains it like this:

GRAVEDIGGER 1

Give me leave. Here lies the water: good. Here stands
the man: good. If the man go to this water and drown
himself, it is *he* goes. But if the water come to him
and drown him, he drowns not himself. He that is not
guilty of his own death...shortens not his own life.

*(The second GRAVEDIGGER stares at him blankly, try-
ing to figure out the logic. Finally...)*

GRAVEDIGGER 2

I like thy wit well.

*(They go back to shoveling imaginary dirt. HAMLET
and HORATIO enter and watch them.)*

HAMLET

What man dost thou dig this for?

GRAVEDIGGER 2

For no man, sir.

HAMLET

What woman then?

GRAVEDIGGER 1

For none, neither.

HAMLET

Who is to be buried in it?

GRAVEDIGGER 1

One that was a woman, sir, but, rest her soul, she's dead.

HAMLET

How absolute the knave is. How long hast thou been gravemaker?

GRAVEDIGGER 1

Since that very day that young Hamlet was born—he that is mad, and sent into England.

HAMLET

Ay, marry, why was he sent into England?

GRAVEDIGGER 1

Why because he was mad. He shall recover his wits there. Or if he do not, 'tis no great matter there.

HAMLET

Why?

GRAVEDIGGER 1

'Twill not be seen in him there. There, the men are as mad as he.

ERIC. Now, see? Shakespeare makes these funny jokes. The gravedigger is in Denmark, but the play is being played to English audiences. And he INSULTS the English with his joke.

SAM. He coulda been on *Comedy Central*!!

*(A funeral procession comes down the aisle of the thea-
tre from the back toward the stage, carrying a body
wrapped in funeral sheets. If possible, there can be some
chanting to pull the audience focus from the stage to the
back of the house.)*

HAMLET
     But soft awhile! Here comes the king, the queen, the
     courtiers.
     Who is this they follow? Crouch we awhile and mark.

*(HAMLET and HORATIO move into the shadows. The
GRAVEDIGGERS make way for the procession.)*

LAERTES
     Lay her in the earth,
     And from her fair and unpolluted flesh
     May violets spring.

GERTRUDE
     Sweets to the sweet, farewell!
     I hoped thou should have been my Hamlet's wife.

HAMLET *(whispering)*
     What, the fair Ophelia??

LAERTES
     Hold off the earth awhile,
     Till I have caught her once more in mine arms.

*(LAERTES falls to his knees and takes the sheet-covered
body in his arms. HAMLET steps forward.)*

HAMLET
> What is he whose grief
> Bears such an emphasis?
> This is I, Hamlet the Dane.

LAERTES
> The Devil take thy soul!

(LAERTES and HAMLET fight. The crowd shouts for them to stop. They pull them apart.)

HAMLET
> I loved Ophelia!

(HAMLET jerks away and leaves. HORATIO runs after him. All exit except CLAUDIUS and LAERTES.)

CLAUDIUS
> Strengthen your patience.
> We'll put the matter to the present push.

(CLAUDIUS and LAERTES exit. The STORYTELLERS jump from their ladders and begin gathering the tombstones and tossing them off stage.)

ERIC. So the king sets up this sword fight between Laertes and Hamlet. He acts like it's just a friendly game of swordplay...

SAM. But really, he wants Hamlet dead, so he's arranged to have...what?...on the tip of Laertes' sword. What? Pop quiz.

JEN. First one who says it gets a free trip to London. Starts with a "P."

(The STORYTELLERS goad the audience into saying "Poison.")

ERIC. Good job. Oh. The trip to London? K-I-D-D-I-N-G.

SAM. Horatio is kinda worried about Hamlet because Laertes is one heck of a good sword fighter. The Bomb, in fact. Hamlet tells him to chill.

HAMLET
    There is a special providence in the fall of a sparrow.
    If it be now, 'tis not to come; if it be not to come, it
    will be now. The readiness is all.

(The king, queen, LAERTES and all the court come on stage.)

CLAUDIUS
    Come, Hamlet, come and take this hand from me.

(He puts LAERTES' hand into HAMLET's.)

HAMLET
    Give me your pardon, sir. I have done you wrong.

LAERTES
    I do receive your offered love
    And will not wrong it.

HAMLET
     Give us the foils.

(They begin a sword fight which goes down the aisles, into the theatre, so that the audience has to turn in their seats sometimes to see them. If possible, have percussion mark each strike of a wooden sword. As they go, there are interjections.)

ERIC. So while they fight, Claudius puts a large pearl into a cup of wine. But it's no ordinary pearl.

CLAUDIUS
     Hamlet, this pearl is thine. Give him the cup.

HAMLET
     Set it by awhile.

(They continue to fight. HAMLET strikes LAERTES.)

CLAUDIUS
     A hit, a very palpable hit! Our son shall win!

(GERTRUDE lifts the cup to toast HAMLET's hit. CLAUDIUS jumps up.)

CLAUDIUS
     Gertrude, do not drink!!

GERTRUDE
     I will, my lord.

(GERTRUDE drinks from the cup.)

CLAUDIUS *(to himself)*
>It is the poisoned cup. It is too late.

HAMLET
>Come, Laertes.
>I pray you, pass with your best violence.

LAERTES
>Have at you now!!

(They fight; LAERTES sword wounds HAMLET and in the scuffle, they exchange swords, and HAMLET wounds LAERTES.)

ERIC. So the poisoned sword has wounded both men now and suddenly the queen falls.

GERTRUDE
>The drink. O, my dear Hamlet! The drink. I am poisoned.

SAM. OK. The next part is rated PG-13 because everyone goes down. It's worse than *Scream 9* and *Halloween 16* combined.

(LAERTES falls.)

LAERTES
>I am justly killed with mine own treachery.
>Hamlet, thou art slain.

In thee there is not half an hour's life.
The treacherous instrument is in thy hand
Envenomed. Thy mother's poisoned.
The king. The king's to blame.

HAMLET *(turning on CLAUDIUS)*
Then venom, to thy work!

(He wounds CLAUDIUS. Then grabs the poisoned cup and forces CLAUDIUS to drink it.)

HAMLET
Here, thou incestuous, murderous, dam-ned Dane.

(CLAUDIUS dies.)

LAERTES
He is justly served.
Exchange forgiveness with me, noble Hamlet.

HAMLET
Heaven make thee free of it. I follow thee.
I am dead, Horatio. Thou livest.
Report me and my cause aright
To the unsatisfied.

(HORATIO grabs the cup to drink some poison himself. HAMLET stops him.)

HAMLET
If thou didst ever hold me in thy heart,

Absent thee from felicity awhile
To tell my story. The rest is silence. *(HAMLET dies.)*

HORATIO
Now cracks a noble heart.
Good night, sweet prince,
And flights of angels sing thee to thy rest.

(The STORYTELLERS climb down from their ladders and walk among the dead bodies.)

JEN. What did we tell you? Horatio's the only one left standing.

SAM. I mean, there's a guy named Fortinbras who comes in and takes over the kingdom. A good guy.

ERIC. But basically all the Hamlets are gone.

JEN. Plus, Polonius, Ophelia and Laertes.

SAM. I mean...that's a whole lot of dying. Horatio's gonna be the loneliest guy in town.

ERIC. And here's the thing that Shakespeare's always sayin'—in all his plays. Bad stuff always happens when greed and jealousy and fear and envy—junk like that—get outta hand.

JEN. I mean, think how different this stage would look right now if Claudius hadn't envied his brother's crown and his brother's wife.

SAM. And then let that feeling get so big he decided to KILL over it.

ERIC. Think if he had just talked it over with a friend. Seen the castle counselor. Worked it out.

JEN. Yeah. Everybody might still be alive!!!

SAM. And Horatio wouldn't have to suck it up and be lonely and brave.

ERIC. So...Bill Shakespeare is now a ghost himself, but if he were here, he'd probably say..."watch the mean stuff." Don't kill anybody. Not even with words.

JEN. Then go out and celebrate your life. Like all week long.

SAM. Give us your hands, as the Bard would say.

(The three STORYTELLERS start clapping their hands over their heads in rhythm. They prod the audience to join them.)

ERIC. Come on!! Bring these guys back to life!

(The "dead" actors begin getting up and clapping. Music starts and the actors do some sort of joyful dance, maybe to harpsichord or harp music. They end by bowing to one another. Smiling and waving to the audience.*

Curtain call.)

THE END

---

* Ideally, the STORYTELLERS will have worked the audience up so that the dance flows right into a curtain call, then back into a dance...through the auditorium, dancing and interacting with the audience.

A WORD ABOUT PRODUCTION DESIGN

Think child's pick-up game. Cut-off broomsticks for swords, a drumstick strike on a trash can lid for the sound of clashing swords, cut-out cardboard for crowns, ladders for the castle parapet. A painted SEAL OF THE KING can suggest the castle, which is basically where all the action takes place.

Everything should come out of the imaginations of the kids and what's at hand—including basic costumes. DON'T RENT FANCY COSTUMES. Basic black pants and black shirts, which a child can bring from home, should be the pallet from which creation begins. Then add a bright scarf and skirt for the queen, something metallic-looking for the king, fake flowers for Ophelia's hair and a pretty skirt. Simple. Stuff they can scavenge from home.

I've been involved in high- and low-end productions of these plays and, believe me, an overly ornate production hurts the effect. It should all look like children pulling together their version of the story.

A note about helmets for the two guards. A plastic gallon milk container is ideal: cut off the spout and about two inches of the carton; cut off the front where the handle is (for the person's face); cut four lines up from the bottom about two inches (the plastic will curl out); color with grey metallic paint (for use on plastic). VOILA!! A medieval helmet!

Safe swordplay: use wooden swords—no sharp, pointy ends. The basics are thrusting and blocking the thrust. Plan it like the steps of a dance and have them rehearse it before every performance.

PROP LIST

3 stepladders
Helmet for Old Hamlet
6 or 7 wooden swords (half broomsticks will do)
2 foils (thinner swords)
Plastic flowers (Ophelia's mad scene)
2 crowns
Briefcase or satchel—Laertes
2 chairs (thrones)
1 book—Hamlet
Large picture of the Globe Theatre in London
2 large ferns
A pair of oversized binoculars
Vial of poison
1 arras (a small, imitation Oriental rug will do)
5 or 6 tombstones (cardboard or foam board)
2 shovels
Funeral sheet—Ophelia
Big, round pearl
2 goblets or cups

DIRECTOR'S NOTES

DIRECTOR'S NOTES

DIRECTOR'S NOTES

DIRECTOR'S NOTES

DIRECTOR'S NOTES